A Student- Athlete's Guide to Excellence

Contents

Introduction   2

Benefits of Excelling   7

Define Excel   12

Goals   16

Prioritizing and Time Management   23

Excel in the Classroom   26

Excel in your Sport   35

Extra Curriculars   45

Financials   48

Having a Social Life   54

Tips   58

Introduction

Congratulations on taking another step toward greatness by opening this book! Whether you are a student- athlete, coach, or a parent willing to help your child excel, you've come to the right place. This book will provide a solid foundation on how you can excel as a student- athlete. No, this book will not teach you calculus or how to hit a homerun, but this will be the book that prepares you to tackle the journey of being an athlete attending school. If you haven't heard, it's not easy. Your day is filled with obstacles many other students will never know of or completely understand. There will be long and difficult days. This book will make those days easier and in some cases avoidable. I can tell you first hand that being a student- athlete is extremely rewarding and enjoyable. For my readers just starting college, these next four years will be incredible. And to those who have experienced part of the journey and are looking to improve upon yourself; this book might make your remaining years if school even more enjoyable. To whoever my readers are, this book is your guide to exceling as a student- athlete.

My name is John Brocious. I'm writing this because I have experienced life as a student- athlete and feel like I can help the thousands of student- athletes out there looking to help themselves. I've managed to obtain two degrees throughout college while playing a sport, participating in extra- curricular clubs, and working throughout college. Let me give you a brief background on myself.

I went to Triton Regional High School in Runnemede, NJ. At Triton I played football and baseball. I participated in clubs such as the Spanish Club and Business Club. I even worked at my aunt's dance studio once I could drive. I managed to make plenty of friends that I keep in touch with to this day. I absolutely loved my time in high school. My years at Triton helped solidify my desire to pursue being a college athlete.

I'm willing to bet my story is not the same as yours. However, I think you'll be able to relate to some of the broader aspects of my life. Toward the end of my junior year, I started the process of searching for colleges. At the end of my senior year baseball season, I chose to go to Gloucester County College (now Rowan College at Gloucester County). This is where my college journey began in the fall of 2011.

I went to Gloucester County for two years. They might have been the best two years of my life. I was a baseball player on one of the best junior college teams in the country (we got ourselves a world series ring to prove it). People knew me as an athlete, but my teammates and other athletes knew that baseball was only the tip of the iceberg. My teammates knew that keeping our grades up was necessary to continue playing. I knew I wanted to succeed in the classroom just as much as I wanted to on the field. Now even those reading who might not have ever played a sport probably know what devotion it takes to keep a high GPA. You may also know that playing a sport requires plenty of hours throughout the day too. Again, only part of the iceberg. When I wasn't going to class or practicing on the field I was involved in several other activities. For one, I worked. No, I didn't have a 40-hour work week. I worked part time, odd jobs. My first two years of college I did plenty of landscaping, writing essays for other students, working at the dance studio, and even cleaning homes. For our Florida baseball trip fundraiser, I worked for the Philadelphia Eagles on their game days. During the times I wasn't practicing, going to class, or working I was hanging out with friends. I should note too that I was involved in a business club called DECA. I'm not here to write you a sob story about how busy my life was as a student- athlete. In fact, I want you to know that I enjoyed all of this. I was doing things I liked doing. And if I was doing something I didn't enjoy, I knew it was for a great reason. I'm telling you it's possible to do all of this and still excel as an athlete, as a student, and as a person.

The following three years I kept a similar schedule. I went to class, played my sport, worked, participated in clubs, and had a social life. After GCC I went to Florida Atlantic for a semester. Again, I kept the same type of schedule. The spring of 2014 I transferred to Philadelphia University (now called Jefferson University). I stayed at Philadelphia University for a year and a half while partaking in whatever I could. After I was done playing at Philadelphia University, I finished my degree online with Southern New Hampshire University. My schedule at Southern New Hampshire University was much different than most of you will experience. I coached at Philadelphia University, worked as a baseball instructor, and was training to play baseball professionally for the upcoming season all while attending online school. I was also part of a group called National Society of Leadership and Success.

So, there you have it. A brief glimpse into a five-year period of my life I will never forget because I managed to excel and create an awesome experience for myself. To fit five years of college would be nearly impossible. I wish you could share my experience with all of you, but since I cannot, I am going to help you create your own incredible experience.

As I said before, this will probably not be your life. However, you may experience something like what I have. I want to help you succeed in what thousands of people go through each day. Your days as a student- athlete can be a blast all while excelling in what you do. Allow this book to help you, help yourself.

Why Do We Benefit from Excelling?

- You open yourself up to so many more opportunities in life.

Think about how exceling opens you up to more opportunities. The star of any sport you can think of is treated a little differently than his or her teammates, aren't they? They might be the ones invited to play up on a better/ older team. They might meet more people on the count of peoples' recognition of their greatness. Now think about the smartest person in your school. You know their name, right? So does everyone else. People walk around wishing they were as smart as that person. This is the person people trust to help solve their problems. Teachers probably treat them a little bit differently too, don't they? Maybe it's as simple as this person explaining how they do things or it might even be them getting more freedom than everyone else. This student might catch certain breaks on a bad day when other people don't. How about at work? Who is the best employee you know? Their schedule is probably ideal for them. Maybe they get to pick when their break is rather than being told, or get the first choice when it comes to days off. Who is the first person you think will get that big promotion or increase in wages?

It's undeniable that those who stand out in what they do are rewarded through more opportunities. Before you move on, think about the times where you excelled and how it has benefitted you.

- You will be remembered. Leave a legacy.

Do you want to be remembered? Stand out? Be the star of your team, ace all your classes, make a living, and be somebody your peers look up to? If you haven't felt the satisfaction of being incredible, I encourage you to try it. Be the person your friends want to be. I think it's a feeling you would never want to give up. People remember those who exceled. And this is not just for the athlete in you. The student in you can be something you're known for too. You'll be remembered by the school rather than just your team. Coaches, teachers, employees, and friends will mention your name for years to come in such a positive light that your legacy will glow.

- Personal Connections and Excellence Recognition

It does not matter what type of person you are, if you're exceling in what you do, you can meet vast amounts of people. What you do with those opportunities is up to you, but the opportunities will present themselves. People recognize you for being top notch and will want you to meet others to show them what you're about. Think about a teacher who has the valedictorian in their class. You don't think they show that person off to other teachers and possibly even professionals in certain fields. If you haven't witnessed it first- hand yet, you might soon: who does coach introduce to the team's alumni? I'm guessing the team's stand out player. The truth is, these personal connections could lead to nothing or they could lead to everything for you. The more people you meet, the better chance you have of a connection helping you in the future. For those of you who are not aware of why connections are crucial to your life, let me enlighten you. When you've acquired your degree, and begin searching for your career, your personal connections will lead you to live your ideal lifestyle. Throughout college you might hear the term "networking" to describe this. The athletes who will move on to play professionally will use a personal connection that will lead them to a better situation, team, or even salary. Our world is a combination of what you know and who you know. There are opportunities that will present themselves for those who excel; much more than those who do not when we consider personal connections and excellence recognition.

- Resume Builder

I'm going to keep this paragraph simple. Show me a resume with an academic and athletic award on it and compare that to a person without any awards. Put yourself in a CEO's shoes and tell me who you would hire.

- More Enjoyable than being mediocre or failing

Close your eyes and think back to a time you performed your best in your sport. How'd that feel? Was there ever a time you were the best kid on your team or close to being the best? Tell me how that felt too. How about in school, remember getting an A on a test? Felt great, right? How about when report cards came out and your grades were better than some of the other students. Let's look at this from a team standpoint. How did it feel winning a championship or being on the best team around? I know personally, I remember how much fun it was playing on the great teams. The point I'm trying to make here is that life is better when you're exceling. Those who have left home to go to college, think about what it will be like to call home with news that you're doing awesome at school. Or think of what it will be like to tell your family how great you're doing around the holidays. There are endless examples of how great it is to excel.

- Be a Role Model

Some of us are lucky enough to have people look up to us. Those with younger siblings understand. It's a great feeling when your younger brother and sister want to grow up and be like you. Excel like you have. Others might have the chance to be a role model to a Little League team or youth group playing a sport. You might not know this, but you are part of molding a younger person's life. Think about that before heading to the next chapter. You have the power to mold another person's life because you have chosen to excel at what you do.

Define Excel

No, this is not the computer program you've used in computer class. Excel is defined as "be exceptionally good at or proficient in an activity or subject. Some synonyms that pop up are: excellent, outstanding, and shine. These are some incredible words to have mentioned with your name. But what does it mean to you? This book is written for you, so how do you define "excel"?

For me it meant to try to be the best at whatever I was doing. That's not the exact definition, but that's how I thought of the word. The truth is, I was really never the best at anything I did. There were better baseball players in the world, smarter students with better grades, and probably better employees than me. There are billions of people in the world, and only one gets to be the best in whatever area you are thinking. Even that person is subject to objection by those arguing for others who are the best. Although I knew I wasn't the best, I worked to be that person who was. My shortcomings lead me to excel in everything I was doing. I was excellent, outstanding, and at times shined in what I was doing.

I don't want you to feel immense pressure to be perfect at what you do every time you do it. Nobody gets every question right in the classroom. Nobody plays a full season of their sport without making a mistake. It's all part of the process. You might not be the absolute best at what you do. But it is possible to excel at what you do. This book isn't about being the best. This book is about exceling. I've left you some wiggle room to be a standout and not be the best. In that same notion, your goal is to be better than the norm. A person who excels in school might not have a 4.0 GPA every semester. But that person who excels at school is close to it. They are not perfect, but they are right there with the best. And maybe some years they are the best. An athlete who excels in their sport might not be the best player on the team every game. But you know that athlete is going to be one of the best contributors to that team every time they play. This is a person who you can generally always count on to stand out above the rest of the group.

Competition is relative to the word excel. If life hasn't hit you with this lesson yet consider yourself lucky or find a new rock to live under in the real world. Life is a competition. Each day we are compared to our peers. Do you want to be the team MVP or the 15th runner up? Not everyone gets a promotion in the real world; only those at the top. Scholastic awards like Valedictorian and Salutatorian, Dean's list, and Honor Roll only goes out to those students who _____. Competition is a huge part of our world. Whether we like it or not, we must rise above the competition to be rewarded more than others. We must excel if we want to live life better than others. If you want to live an average life, the world cannot wait to accept you. Most of the world lives this way. There is an abundance of people who easily fit in with everyone else. Again, I'd like to revert back to who do you want to be? Where do you want to fit in with the world?

Let me make something clear. Competition is fierce. Life is a competition. However, if you're on the golf team, the world will not expect you to excel on the tennis court. If you're an astrophysicist, the world will not expect you to excel as the president of marketing for a major corporation. You do not need to excel in everything known to mankind because it is impossible to do so. Excel in what is relative to you. Most of you reading this are student-athletes. If you're not, that's okay too because this is a valuable lesson. Excel at what you are doing. This means if you are a waiter/waitress at a restaurant, excel in that. Athletes, excel in your sport. Students (this is broad), excel at being a student. You are part of a classroom and part of a school that gets graded on performance. Excel while performing what you do. I wrote this book for a specific audience, but this desire can be for anybody out there who lives and breathes.

Now it is time for you to decide your definition of excel. Ask yourself questions like this:

1.   What am I doing?

This might be playing a sport, attending school, working, a passionate hobby, etc.

2.   Who am I competing against?

Who is doing what you are doing? Is it a team or an individual?

3.   Who is already exceling in this already?

This might be who you look up to. It could even be a great opponent. Maybe it's a friend. What are their qualities? How can you take what they do and use it to your benefit?

Goals

This is a great time to consider your goals as well. Without goals, we are blindly heading down a path of existence without direction. Think of setting goals as mapping out a road trip. It is tough to get where you want to be without knowing where you are going. Planning to reach your goals may be easier said than done.

Goals can be broken down into long- term and short- term. Your long- term goals might include our word "excel". You want to excel in the classroom, excel in your sport, or excel at work. Some of you might be seeking out an award or championship with your team. Some people might see a certain GPA they want to obtain. When considering a goal, think S.M.A.R.T. Specific, Measurable, Attainable, Relevant, and Time- bound. Your goal should be specific as possible. Ability to measure your goal will help you realize what needs to be done. This goal should be something within reason. The "R" will relate to your "why". And this goal should have timetables to keep you going. Whatever your goal is, you should map out how you are going to reach it.

I've always thought of my long- term goals as this: what do I desire the most? For me, I've always wanted to play baseball professionally. Every morning, I woke up thinking about that. Throughout college, I always wanted to reach a GPA of over 3.5. As an employee, whatever I was doing, I had a variety of goals in terms of how I want my boss, co- workers, and customers to see me and I always gave myself a certain monetary goal to reach. Socially, I wanted to be a person people liked to be around.

Keeping things simple, I am going to talk about our goals as a student, an athlete, and an employee.

STUDENT

I cannot stress how important it is to do well in school. Your time as an athlete will end one day. Soaking up as much information as you can, will help you as long as you are alive. We talked about long term goals as a student already. Those shooting for a certain GPA or academic award, perfect. This is a S.M.A.R.T goal.

How are we going to get there? We need to map out our short- term goals. A goal of reaching a 3.5 GPA at the end of the semester is a great start. Now where do you have to be come mid- term reports? What will your test scores have to look like? Your class participation grade should look like what? Turning in assignments will need to happen how often? Class attendance will have to be at what number? There are hundreds of questions you can ask yourself when considering short- term goals.

Taking a step further we can assess ourselves weekly. Ask yourself the same questions as before. Then, we can assess ourselves daily. You don't have to go crazy with tracking every single element of your classes. But it is possible to set small goals for yourself every day. I'll give you an example.

I want a 3.5 GPA at the end of the semester. This means I need to get mostly A's and some B's in my classes. At the end of the mid- term I would like to have a 3.5 GPA or above. Each week I have 10 total classes. I want my attendance to be perfect. Each day I have class I want to participate in a discuss or answer a question at least one time. I want to turn in all my homework. In class, I want to take notes on whatever the professor is teaching today. My tests and quizzes should be at a B+ range or higher. Some of these guidelines are easy enough to answer with a simple yes or no. "Did I accomplish this?". At the end of my days, weeks, mid- term, and semester I can track my progress on my goal.

ATHLETE

We can use a similar approach as an athlete. We must decide on a S.M.A.R.T goal. This could be wining the team MVP, earning All- American, an even accomplish something statistically. Find your long- term, S.M.A.R.T goal first. Next, we move into short- term goals.

Let's ask ourselves some questions. How is our practice attendance? Did I put in extra work outside of practice? Did I get stronger in the weight room? Am I quicker, faster, more agile, or more explosive? Did I recover properly? Did I eat right? What was my focus like at practice? What was my performance like at practice? How did today's game go? How have I played this week, month, year? Again, there are so many questions we can ask ourselves to keep our short- term goals on track.

Keep track of these answers to your questions. You can rate yourself each day. Every practice, lift, stretch, run, etc. is a chance to review where you are at on the short- term goals list. I'm going to give you another example as an athlete. Let me stick to baseball because I'm not going to pretend I know a different sport better than those who play it.

I want to win our team MVP at the end of the year. I'm using this example because it covers more than just performance. Did I show up to every practice I could? Did I lift, run, stretch, etc. every time I was required to? Did I put in extra work on my own time to better myself and my teammates? Did I help a teammate or multiple teammates get better today? Was my focus at practice MVP caliber? Was my effort the best on the team? Did I lead by example today? What was my game performance like? Personally, I would grade each of my questions with letter grades. Once I got into a routine, grading myself became easier. My lifestyle changed. Instead of shooting for an A grade on questions like "How was my focus at practice?", I started answering the questions, did I perform my best today? This covered everything I did. I knew how to focus, I knew how to lead, and I knew how I needed to perform. If I did my best that day, I was on pace to accomplish my goal.

EMPLOYEE

For those of you who will be working and looking to excel, this section is for you. I don't care if you are the owner of the best casino in Las Vegas or you are working in the fast food industry; setting goals is crucial to success. Many of you reading this might be taking on lower wage jobs to survive your college years. I applaud your effort to live independently while filling your schedule with school and athletics as well. But, getting a job is only the beginning. This book is about exceling in everything you do, so why would a part- time job be any different? We talked about some of the benefits for those who excel in the workplace earlier. Creating long and short- term goals is the right step to exceling at work.

There is a vast array of jobs out there. I want to provide you with a broad guideline to long and short- term goals to excel in any job you might have. You've set a S.M.A.R.T goal already. So, let's start by asking ourselves questions. Did I show up every day I was required to? Was I on time? Did I perform what is expected of me? Did I go above and beyond to do my job better than most people? How was my focus and effort? For those looking to make a certain amount of money: did I work enough hours? Did I make enough phone calls or send emails?

Think about how this is relative to your job. You can track this daily, weekly, monthly, quarterly, semi-annually, and yearly if you would like. Some jobs might even allow you to track progress hourly or by the minute. Once you've created the norm to excel, you can start asking the question "Did I perform the best I could today?". You might not be the best employee every single day. But those who excel at their job are top of the pack most days. Put yourself in your boss' shoes. What is he looking for? Have you met his/her requirements and have done better?

No matter what you are setting goals in remember:

1. Set a S.M.A.R.T goal.

2. Ask yourself questions relevant to your goal.

3. Set short- term goals.

4. Reflect on your performance toward these goals.

Goal setting does not have to be difficult. Set aside some time to sit and think about what you want to accomplish. These goals could change your life. They could set you on a path to something incredible that others may only dream of.

Prioritizing/ Time Management

The chapter in the book is essential to your success. I've found that many coaches and professors see student-athletes struggling with this the most when entering college. Most of you are going to have more responsibility than ever before. This could be your first time living on your own. You might be in a new environment with new people. You've been placed out of your comfort zone in an atmosphere that requires you to do well no matter what your circumstance is. Time management and prioritizing will help you not only survive this, but excel in it.

First, let's discuss prioritizing. This will allow you to manage your time. Prioritizing is meant to help you see what is more than important than other aspects in your life. Sit and think about what is important to you. For myself, I've come up with a simple list: Family, school, baseball, work, social/ leisure time. Your list may differ. Once you've created a list, talk with those close to you about it. They might provide feedback, but may also help you stick to it. No matter what your list is, spend some time reflecting on it. This is your life, take it seriously.

Once we've prioritized, we can move on to time management. This is knowing the aspects of your life and how they will interact with one another according to time. One of the best things you can do for yourself is to KEEP A SCHEDULE. Carry a planner around with you. Keep a planner in your room. Write things down for the future as often as you can. Your day is filled with so many different activities; keeping track of everything is nearly impossible without writing things down. This paragraph alone could help you excel in everyday life.

Taking five minutes each day to think and write out your tomorrow is the easiest and most rewarding thing you can do for your time management. This only requires effort and some time. Write out what you are going to do from the time you wake up, until you are done everything you needed to do. If you don't have a calendar, use a planner. If you don't have a planner use Post- it notes. If you don't have Post- it notes, use a shred of paper or put your schedule on your phone. Keeping track of your life is incredibly easy to do and more than affordable. There is no reason this cannot be done.

After your schedule is written down, try your best to stick to it. Of course, there will be days where your schedule changes in the middle of the day. That's fine to change your day when necessary. When I say stick to your schedule, I'm asking you to not skip out on the necessary elements of it. If you've written down exercise from 12- 1, don't skip out because you don't feel like doing it. Your motivation to excel the night before can do wonders for you on days you don't feel like exceling. The truth is, you don't HAVE to do anything on your schedule. If you remember to breath today, you are going to live. What will it take for you to excel? Stick to what it takes to be the person you and everybody else wants to be.

Excel in the Classroom

If you are just entering college, you will find that the smartest students don't always earn the best grades. Those who are dedicated to learning will benefit the most. This means that those of you who make a commitment to learning will most likely succeed. Your professors (whether you want to believe it or not) are not out to fail you. These are people that have dedicated their life to learning and would like to share the knowledge with you. With that being said, I'd like to give you some pointers on how to excel in the classroom.

RESPECT YOUR PROFESSORS

- Be on time
    - When you are late, you show the professor that your time is more valuable than theirs. How would that make you feel?

- Do not be disruptive
    - Speaking while the professor or a classmate is speaking falls under this. Cell phones ringing are distracting. Opening that family size bag of potato chips from your backpack is disruptive.

Anything that takes the professor's or students' focus from the lesson is disruptive.

- Focus on the lesson
  - ➢ This means you should not pull out your cell phone to check your social media sites during class. Don't pull out work from another class and start working on it. Reading a book that isn't what the professor asked you to read counts as not focusing on the lesson.

- Have some manners
  - ➢ Hopefully mom and dad have already given you some insight, but just in case, let me. When you walk into a class and you make eye contact with your professor, say hello. It will go a long way when the other 22 students say nothing. When the professor gives you something, say thank you. If you've fallen short on anything above, apologize. Own up to your mistakes. This might mean walking into class late (I know situations come up, professors do too) and quietly apologizing while walking to your seat. Honesty is another way to show respect. Didn't read a passage for your homework? "I'm sorry professor, I didn't read the pages you asked me

to, it won't happen again". You will earn their respect with polite honesty. You would barely go out of your own way for any of these, but they show your respect for the professor. I'm sure the professor will treat you with the same respect back.

If there comes a point where you are not sure of how to act, put yourself in the professor's shoes. What would you want to see from your students in this situation? Unless my parents or siblings start teaching, you will know your professor than I will. Adjust to your circumstance and do your best to be respectful.

COMMIT TO YOUR SCHOOLWORK

On top of respecting your professor, there are some guidelines to help you with the actual schoolwork you will have this year.

- Focus (again)
  - This means focusing while you're in class. You might think you can ace every class by checking the lecture slides later. Focusing in class will probably save you the time of re-learning the lesson when you're at home again with the ability to ask questions that you need

answered. Watch how easy your homework assignments are when you pay attention to the whole lecture.

- Take notes

    ➢ You are busy which means your brain is too. Taking notes will help you avoid forgetting things. Find a note taking routine that works for you. You don't have to write down every little thing the professor says. Write down what is necessary. Most of the information you take in will be forgotten, write down notes as a reminder of what you learned.

- Turn in your assignments

    ➢ Professors see this as a chance to grade you. Which for you, means a chance to excel. Don't get a 0 on something you could have put minuscule effort into to earn a much higher grade. You don't want to be kicking yourself come the end of the semester because you missed an "A" by 2 points when you could've just turned in your assignments.

- Participate

- ➢ This is your time to show the class that you've been paying attention and want to be there. Whether you truly you want to be in class is a different story, but acting like you want to be there could lead you to a better grade. Put yourself in a professor's shoes. At the end of the semester whose grade would you bump up: the student who participated in class, or the person who didn't contribute to the discussions at all?

- Sit near the front

  - ➢ Plain and simple. Most of the classes you've ever attended where students could choose their seat; who usually sits in the front? Those who excel. Let that be you. It might be cool sitting in the back. You'll look like the person who doesn't care about class, and I'm sure that's still cool to college kids. But when you've moved out of your parents' house, have a great job, and take vacations because you exceled in school, guess who will be more popular? And again, I am going to ask you to put yourself in your professor's shoes. Which student presents themselves as someone willing to excel?

- Avoid distractions
  - We talked about not being the distraction, but we also want to avoid them too. This means avoid sitting next to somebody constantly talking. Anybody keeping you from focusing is not helping you excel in your work. They are indirectly making the class much more difficult in the long- run for you. Yes, it can be a lot of fun sitting next to a teammate or a friend, but make sure they know the deal – you are going crush this class and they cannot stop that from happening. Another common distraction is your phone. You're going to keep it on you, which is fine, but turn it on sleep mode. Your friends texting you won't help you ace this class.

ADDITIONAL TIPS

- Except responsibility. Do not blame the professor or a certain class for your mistakes and failures. You are going to make mistakes, own up to it. This is a huge part of growing up.

- Know what type of learner you are. Some people learn best visually, in writing, or from listening. If you must draw pictures, make charts, write down key points, create verbal cues, etc. then do whatever you must to excel.

- Create an environment at home or in your dorm to do your homework and to study. Go someplace quiet and clean that can help you concentrate. This might also mean heading to the school library.

- Write down what is required before you return for the next class. Write down all homework assignments and things you will need to do while not in class.

- Try to set a schedule to complete homework. Set aside an hour or two each night and take care of all the work you need to. You might not need to use all of this time, but it will feel like a treat when you get a day off or get done early.

- ASK FOR HELP. Use every resource available to you. I struggled with Calculus my freshman year of college. The best thing I have ever done for myself was getting help from a peer tutor. If a professor cannot explain everything in the time of a class, ask for help elsewhere. A professor might even be able to direct you to somebody or an online resource. Whatever help you find will be extremely valuable.

- Again, put yourself in your professor's shoes. It will help you understand what it takes to excel in each class you'll ever take.

- Remember the end goal. I'm not going to tell you that every single class you take will grab your curiosity and keep you excited to learn every aspect of the subject. It won't. Just like in life there will be certain things you must learn or do to excel in your life. Keeping the end goal in mind will help you get through a monotone instructor or a subject you don't care for so much.

- To the point above, try your best to see the best in each subject. Think about the better parts of the workforce that use that subject to benefit their lives. I hated learning about statistics, but when I read about the professionals who use it and what they do, it became a little more interesting.

In this entire chapter, I did not bring up any points on how smart you need to be to excel in a class. I gave you starting points to help you learn. From what I've seen in the four colleges I've been to, you can pass most of the classes you take by just showing up and turning in homework. You are here to excel though. Take the necessary steps to put yourself in the best position to do so. You don't always have to be the smartest in the class to do the best. Most of the time you must be willing to be the best.

Excel in Your Sport

This is the chapter many of you have been waiting for. I want to start this chapter by saying how fortunate you are to be playing a sport as a college athlete. Even high schoolers out there, this goes for you too. Some people don't have the ability to play a sport. Some people don't have the ability to play it well enough to be considered a college athlete. So, before I get started on how to excel in your sport, take some time to reflect on how fortunate you are. Speaking as a former collegiate athlete, this WILL BE one of the best times of your life. You will meet people that you might not have otherwise. You will learn what it takes to sacrifice certain things to benefit a team, rather than just yourself. You will be a part of something incredible. Many of you can consider yourself in the top tenth percentile in your sport just by making a college roster. Enjoy every second of this journey.

RESPECT YOUR TEAMMATES, COACHES, AND TRAINERS

- Put in your best effort
    - ➢ Anything less than your best is an insult to your team. You're not helping yourself which in turn,

does not help your team. How would you feel if you were giving your best effort and you looked over to see somebody dogging it?

- Arrive early

  - ➢ This means show up a little bit early before you are supposed to. Show your team that this team means more to you than waiting until the last minute to arrive. If you are showing up right on time, you will be less prepared to excel than those who showed up early.

- Have some manners

  - ➢ We talked about this in the classroom. Please, thank you, hello, and goodbye go a long way. Don't be afraid to say hello to Coach. Your coach has a personality too. You're an adult now, be polite. Same thing goes for how you should treat your teammates. This takes just about no effort, but goes a long way to describe you as a person.

- Sacrifice

  - ➢ We're talking about not being selfish here. Sacrifice time and effort to go the extra mile for your team. Stay after practice to help a teammate, take some time to clean up the field before a recruit shows up, volunteer at school events that will help your team's image. This also means not staying up until dawn the night before a game or practice, not drinking alcohol before games or practice, looking out for teammates. There are endless examples of how you can sacrifice. Put the team first, and you will be on the right path to exceling yourself.

COMMIT TO YOUR PERFORMANCE

- Put in the time
    - Exceling in your sport is not going to be a cake walk. This will require not only practice time, but time afterward too. This means getting stronger, eating right, stretching, recovering, and getting better. Your practices are made to make the team better. The time after or before practice will help you personally excel. Let's pretend you have 100 practices in a year. And you stay 1 hour after each practice to work on your game. That's 100 extra hours of work. One hour a day after each practice leads you to be more than four literal days better than those who put in the minimum amount of time.

What's crazy is that 100 practices are not even close to the amount of days you will put toward your sport.

- Work smarter
  - ➢ Make your practices efficient. Stop working on what isn't necessary. Some of you might be going the extra mile in the wrong path. Avoid anything that isn't helping you excel.

- Study your sport
  - ➢ Become a student of the game. There are experts out there. There are professionals to look up to. What are the best in the world doing? Put yourself at and advantage through knowledge.

- Ask for help
  - ➢ Nobody does it all on their own. Questions encourage growth. If you are playing in college, there are likely many people around you willing to help you excel. This extends from coaches to teammates to your parents and possibly to the professionals out there willing to help.

ADDITIONAL TIPS

- Practice
  - This will take up most of your time as an athlete. Practice is crucial to your success in the sport. In practice, focus is key. Don't let your brain wander off while you or a teammate is being coached. Communication is important. If you don't understand something, ask your coach. They would much rather have you as a question than screw something up because you were afraid to ask. Again, always give your best effort. You're not going to be lazy during a game, are you?
- Put yourself in your coach's shoes
  - Your coach hopes and wishing for his/her players to excel. What do they want to see? These coaches are there to win. Players exceling will be the backbone to their success. So, what do you need to do for coach to want more players like yourself?
- Work on what you're not great at
  - Warning: this will be frustrating, but so worth it. Don't allow yourself to have a hole in your game. Working on the worst parts

of your game will lead to performance you may never have thought possible before. It won't be easy, it might not be fun, but it will help you excel.

- Make mistakes (Leave your comfort zone)

  - Nothing ever grows in the comfort zone. Trying something new could lead to failures. It could also lead to success like you've never seen. If you are doing everything perfect, then you are not letting yourself work toward a higher ceiling.

- Encourage teammates to excel too

  - This will separate you from many other people. Bringing your teammates along with you to do extra work can help you, them, and the rest of the team. If this is a teammate you're competing with, even better. You have a friend who knows the most about what you need to get better. This bullet point is also what being a leader is all about. Leaders not only help themselves, but help others.

- Embrace competition

- ➢ Competition is there. If you're the best on your team, somebody on a different team is the best on their team too. If you're the best in the country, somebody (the whole country) is waiting to take that title away from you. Accept the fact that competition is there. Use it to your advantage. Let it motivate you. At the very least, compete with yesterday's version of yourself.

- Outside of practice

  - ➢ Recovery is a huge part of performance. Make sure you set aside time to recover properly. This might mean ice baths, heat treatment, or stretching. Nutrition is another crucial part to your success. Junk food is not the solution to exceling in your sport.

- Keep track of yourself, your team, and other teams

  - ➢ See what you've progressed or digressed on. This might mean your play, your strength, speed, or anything else that's measurable. Keep a notebook of what you've learned about your sport and yourself. Write notes about your teammates and other teams. Understanding your teammates can lead to better chemistry. Understanding another team can help you avoid surprises.

- Visualize/ Motivation

  - If you can believe in yourself, you are halfway there. Visualize yourself performing at your best. See yourself doing exactly what you want to. Try this in the morning or during pre- game. Staying motivated isn't always easy. Look for ways to continue your passion for this sport. Sometimes it takes watching videos of yourself, sometimes it takes talking to a teammate or coach, and sometimes it takes watching the sport. Do whatever you can to stay motivated because it can lead you to an even further desire to excel.

- Report/ take care of injuries

  - You have one body, take care of it. Ignoring injuries will lead to disaster. Take care of it now rather than waiting until it is much worse.

- Attention to detail
  - ➤ This is a concept that is relative to life. When your coach is instructing, know the fine details of what they are discussing. Understanding the smallest terms in a conversation can lead to the greatest outcomes. Paying attention to detail also includes: report time, uniform, location, etc.

- Requires no skill
  - ➤ Be the best at what requires no skill. This includes effort, showing up early, staying positive, being a good teammate, coming prepared, etc.

I haven't said anything about how you can work on your sets, your swing, your form, or your passing. I've given you guidelines to help yourself excel in all aspects of your sport. Consider this chapter as building blocks to help you be a stand out in your sport. Remember you are here to excel, the fundamentals matter most when you're preparing yourself to do so.

Extra-Curricular

This short chapter will be about what you can get involved in outside of class and your sport. Fortunately, most colleges and even most high schools in the country have many options with extra- curricular activities. This might mean joining a certain group, club, or even volunteering somewhere. Although this might be a tough commitment, it will be worth it. Being involved in something outside of class and your sport will open you up to some great opportunities to excel as a person.

Although this is not necessary, let's talk about the benefit for those who do decide to participate in something outside of being a student- athlete.

- You will meet new people and make new friends. Never underestimate the power of making a personal connection with people.
- This is a great resume builder. It shows employers you can handle a lot on your plate. This shows you take interest in things outside of your sport too. For those volunteering, I'm sure I don't have to explain to you the benefits as to what it says about you as a person.

- This will add another group of connections you might not have otherwise. The world operates often as not what you know, but who you know. Joining a group outside of the typical people you see will allow you to know those people.
- This could be fun! Join something that interests you. Consider this a hobby if you'd like. Your day is filled with "have- to's", this is your chance to include a "want- to".

Now as a student- athlete, this will not be an easy task. You are committed to school, your team, and maybe even work. Now you are adding on another commitment. I want to give you some tips on how to be a great group member while upholding all of your other responsibilities.

- Be open and honest. Let your new group know what else you have going on. Most people will understand that your other commitments come first. Do everything you can to ensure your new group that although you have these other commitments, you will do whatever you can to make time for this group too.

- Don't take a leadership position unless you absolutely can. Your time will most likely be spent elsewhere. More times than not student- athletes will have to put their group somewhere toward the bottom of their priority list. There is nothing wrong with that. But do not be the person who people look up to and rely on when you know this is not your biggest concern. Take a role in the group that fits your needs as well as the group's.

• Contribute as often as possible. You've made a commitment, right? If you are not contributing to your other priorities, contribute to this group. Don't be lazy on your commitment. While you are there, be the best contributor you possibly can be.

Joining a club or group can be a great way to excel as a student athlete. Remember to keep this in mind while prioritizing your schedule. You may not be able to clear your schedule for this group, but when you can participate, be the best person for the group as you possibly can.

Financials

This chapter in the book might not apply to some of you. To others, this chapter may help you survive college. Money is a huge part of our world, and being a student-athlete doesn't mean you can avoid that fact. For those of you looking to make money and save money while going to school, this chapter is for you.

FINDING WORK

The hardest part of earning money is often trying to find the right job. Some of you might be lucky enough to have a connection. Others, not so much. Here are some tips on finding work.

- Try to work near campus or home

  - An hour commute after a busy day will make you not want to work. Find somewhere that is close and easily accessible. Beware of traffic too. Sitting in traffic for long periods of time will discourage you from wanting to work at your job. This also allows you the option to work more hours due to less travel time.

- Find a job you like doing

- ➢ "Find a job you like, and you'll never work a day in your life". If you can't get hired as a movie critic or video game player or anything else you might like to do; try finding something you wouldn't mind doing for work. Don't make yourself miserable just to make money. The truth is, you will spend a lot of hours at this job. Don't spend those hours wishing you weren't there. If you can't find a job you like at all, try to find a job with a friend. Working with a friend can be fun regardless of what you are doing for work.

- Don't do anything illegal

  - ➢ Do I need to write more on this topic? Just because it's easier, doesn't mean you should do it. Think about the consequences rather than the money.

- Think outside of the box

  - ➢ A 9-5 job will not happen for you until summer or after college. Think of jobs to do on off hours. You play a sport at the college level; coach younger kids in that. Believe it or not, you are considered an expert to people younger than you and to their parents. Do work for your peers. Writing essays, tutoring, and even doing somebody's laundry all semester can lead to some serious money. The best part is that you can be your own boss and work when you want. If you are good at something or like a particular area of work, find a way to work doing that. You don't need to be a multi-million-dollar CEO to start your own little gig. Advertise through social media and bulletin board signs. Get the word out however you can. The bottom line: use your skills and your interests to make money that might be considered not normal.

SAVING MONEY

- Track your money
    - Allow yourself to physically see what your money is doing. What did you spend it on? How much did you earn? It's harder to spend money on useless items when you have to look back and see what you've done.

- Cut back on spending
    - I used to categorize my spending into 3 categories. NEEDS, WANTS, and ENJOYEMENT.

NEEDS were things like food, school supplies, rent, house items, car insurance, etc. Things you need the money for. For most of you it is probably why you are working. WANTS were just what the word means. I don't need it, but I want it. This might've been some extra sport gear, snacks for my room, or new clothes. When you're doing well with earning money, you can afford to spend more on the WANTS. ENJOYMENT might be tough to distinguish from the WANTS. This is usually not a NEED, but it could be just as important sometimes. ENJOYMENT might be spending money on going out with your friends or teammates. Maybe it's a night out at the movie theater or restaurant. If you have the money, try to put ENJOYMENT before the WANTS. ENJOYMENT usually leads to memories that you will never forget. Some of the best money you'll spend is on ENJOYMENT.

- In these three categories, try cut back when you can. If it's possible, cut down the things you need. See if you can survive on less. WANTS will be the easiest to cut back on. ENJOYMENT is a great way to spend your money, but if you're struggling for work, don't do this often. Spend money on ENJOYMENT as a treat to yourself.

- Set goals for yourself

    > Once you know your schedule, NEEDS, WANTS, and how much you'll be making, try to set goals for yourself. Set goals weekly or monthly and stick to them the best you can. If you exceed your goals than you've exceled in something else! Consider yourself a better person for it. We talked about S.M.A.R.T goals in a previous chapter; use the same concept for your money too. Budget yourself. Make sure you will be making more money than you'll be spending.

Money can make you want to pull your hair out at times. Other times, it can bring some ease into your life. As a student- athlete, don't let work consume you. You have four years to be a student- athlete and the rest of your life to work. Don't let this time pass you by stuck at a part-time job when you could be enjoying your time as a student- athlete. Remember to prioritize properly when fitting work into your schedule. Although this may seem unfair that some of you have to work while others don't, it says a lot about you as a person when you can handle money and a job while being a student- athlete. You are a person of many hats; embrace that.

Having a Social Life

You're almost finished this book! And this chapter is something you might be looking forward to. Having a social life is probably the best part of going to college along with playing a sport. Don't let anybody tell you that there is no social life as a college athlete, because that is not true. What most people mean is that there is much less time for a social life than those who are not a student-athlete. If that is what you've heard, they are right. There will be less time for going to parties, hanging out in the cafeteria, and laying around your apartment or dorm with your friends. Although that's true, you will be more likely to create friendships with people you will consider as close as a sibling. And you'll be able to make friends through your teammates. This is a give and take situation. You will enjoy your time as a student- athlete regardless. Maybe even more than those not playing a sport.

PRIORITZE

Make sure you take care of what you need to before your social life. True friends will understand your commitment to excellence and will encourage you to complete everything else before hanging out with your group of friends. Take care of your school work. Do what you need to for your team. For those who have to work, go make that money! Do what's required of your extra-curricular group if you are in one. Having a social life will fall into place. You will see that what you are required to do will allow plenty of free time to hang out with friends. And sometimes what you HAVE to do will lead you to socialize too. Treat your social life as something to look forward to. If you are always hanging out with friends, will you look forward to it in the future? Probably not. Let your social life be a treat to you.

BE RESPONSIBLE

You're not only an adult now, but you have the responsibility of representing those close to you while you are away from home and your team. Don't do anything where people will lose respect for you or those who care about you. Knowing what is right and wrong can solve many of the responsibility issues you'll come across. Is going out drinking the night before a game right or wrong? Is taking this illegal drug right or wrong? It's no secret that under age college students drink alcohol. Do you have to fit the norm? Are you responsible enough to do the right thing under the influence of alcohol? Are you ready to accept the consequences if you are caught or act poorly while under the influence? Do not put yourself at risk of smirching your name or those who you represent.

Being responsible extends to people outside of yourself. Your teammates and friends will not always make the best decisions. Be there for them to help make the right decision. Keep teammates and friends away from disgracing themselves. Keep in mind what is ethically and legally the right decision always. This book is about exceling as a student- athlete which means all that come with it. You are held to a higher standard than most people because of your role at the school. You represent more than just yourself. Consequences you may experience extend further than just yourself.

TAKING ADVANTAGE OF YOUR SITUATION

As an athlete, you are introduced to more people and groups of people than you think. Count your teammates. Then go on and count their friends. Count the players on other teams at your school. You can even count opponents if you are outgoing enough. There are webs upon webs of connections for you to make as an athlete. This means you can expand your groups of friends even further than most people can. On top of that, you have something to talk about with those who might not do what you do. Many people will see a student- athlete as an interesting person because they don't know the ins and outs of an athlete. Take advantage of the ability to hang out with your teammates. You can take advantage of the people you can meet just because of who you are around and who you are.

Take advantage of where you are. If you're living in the dorms at school, meet those who live there too. Living in an apartment complex? Introduce yourself to the other tenants. You go to college; hang out in the common areas occasionally to meet new people. You won't get to do this when you're out of college. Each day you are surrounded by hundreds and sometimes thousands of people your age depending on where you go to school. Maybe every conversation with a stranger won't turn into a friendship. That's okay! You can say you met somebody new and maybe even learn about something you didn't know before. Sometimes a simple "hello" can lead to a friendship or connection you might not have experienced otherwise. Take advantage of where you are.

Tips

It's impossible to cover everything you will experience in college. In the chapters prior to this, I've introduced you to certain steps to help you excel. I want this chapter to cover any gaps I've missed and give you some more tips on how you can excel.

- Find some routine

    - We create a routine to keep us on track. Completing homework at a certain time gives you some guidance on a very important aspect of being a student-athlete. Working out or eating at specific times during the day can lead to a healthy lifestyle. Have a routine with some parts of your life to help you excel.

- Buy a planner

    - I want to reiterate this bullet point from the beginning of the book. Having a planner and using it will help you remember everything you need to. Your days will start to mix together and remembered every detail about what you need to do next will be difficult. A planner will be a great investment for keeping your life together.

- Surround yourself with others looking to excel
    - Hint: this does not have to be a teammate. This can be anybody willing to excel in whatever they do. Your inner circle says a lot about you. Choose these people wisely. Who will benefit you on your quest to stand above and beyond the crowd? Find like-minded people who have a desire to accomplish what you plan to. Don't let a bad environment bring you down.

- Set time aside to recharge
    - If you don't you're going to be overwhelmed. Relax your body and your brain from time to time. Find time to meditate without distraction. Find an activity that calms you and could possibly take you away from the world you're in mentally. Sometimes reading a book, yoga, or listening to music can help you recharge. Exceling as a student- athlete is tough, recharging yourself is necessary.

- Enjoy these next four years

    - You only get this part of your life to do the things you're doing. It's an incredible opportunity. Spend time working hard to reach your goals. Enjoy the fact that you are in the position you're in. Many other people will never get to experience what you are doing. Every day is a chance to enjoy yourself while improving your future.

- Take pictures and keep a journal

    - These years will go by in a flash. Take pictures with friends. Document some major moments in a journal. It doesn't have to be a novel of your day, just write down what you think you'll want to remember one day when you tell your kids about your college years. You might not reap the benefits now, but one day you'll thank me for this one.

- Give it everything you've got

    - Follow this tip because it will lead you to the best life possible. It will make those who care for you proud. Those who know you will think highly of you. Those who will meet you will know they are in the presence of excellence.

www.ingramcontent.com/pod-product-compliance
Lightning Source LLC
Chambersburg PA
CBHW071218240526
45470CB00018B/2072